Special thanks to Dr. Jonathan Cheek, Ph.D.,
professor of psychology at
Wellesley College in Massachusetts.

phase 1:

PANIC ON THE INSIDE, CATASTROPHE ON THE OUTSIDE

contents

phase 2: WHY AM I SHY?

phase 3: WHAT CAN I DO ABOUT IT?

WHY CAN'T I JUST SAY WHAT I'M THINKING? WHAT MAKES MY HANDS TREMBLE AND MY FACE GO BEET RED? WHY DOES MAKING FRIENDS SEEM SO EASY FOR OTHER PEOPLE? WILL I BE THIS SHY FOR THE REST OF MY LIFE?

When you're little, being shy can seem charming. Adults think it's cute to see you blush or run and hide behind the sofa. They like "well-behaved" children who don't interrupt their conversations with annoying jokes or demands, who don't cause trouble with yelling and screaming and wild games.

But now that you're older, it's different. Sure, parents and teachers still like the well-behaved part, especially when comparing you to the more rebellious kids in your class. But then they start bugging you about why you aren't more involved at school, why you don't want to have a birthday party this year, why you're getting such bad grades for class participation, and why you can't entertain Cousin Martin from out of town while they run out to pick up dinner.

The thing is, you're secretly wondering the same things. This social anxiety bit is keeping you on the sidelines, preventing you from living the life you want.

Don't worry—it doesn't have to be this way forever. While everyone is born with a unique personality, we all continue to shift and develop throughout life. You can change things about yourself, if you want to. It's hard—that's true! But we're here to help guide you through it. So let's get started!

i can't talk!

PANIC on the

CATASTROPHE

misunderstood

**everybody's
looking
at me**

IS IT HOT IN HERE?

nside,

trapped inside

on the outside

THE MENTAL VCR

shyness

when you know it's time for a change

Imagine this: your English teacher knows a guy who knows a guy and, long story short, your favorite actor has agreed to come in and speak to your class about getting his start doing community Shakespeare! There he is, right in front of you, the one you've been dying to meet. He's standing a few yards away from you, smiling, just as cool as you've always imagined him.

At first everyone's holding their breath, waiting for him to speak. Then, he starts talking like he's known you his whole life. He makes a joke and everyone laughs. The tension in the room melts away.

You'd love to do theater, just like him. But your parents aren't exactly thrilled with the idea. Being a professional actor is risky. And they probably figure with your personality, you'd never even make it out onstage. You're afraid to even ask for directions! So a career in front of an audience is out of the question. Something with computers . . . that's where you belong. You could stare at a screen all day long without ever having to talk to another person. At the rate you're going, it seems like the only option.

Although . . . you did read in a magazine once that your actor wasn't always so confident and outgoing, that he had to battle a recurring case of stage fright before becoming the celebrity he is today. You'd love to ask him about it: what courses to take, what roles to play, what tricks you can use to conquer your anxieties . . .

Yeah right, like that's going to happen. Once the actor finishes talking, the teacher asks if anyone has a question. A few students shamelessly call out: "What's it like to be rich?" "Can I get your autograph?" Others politely rattle off theater-related questions they'd prepared beforehand.

But not you. You sit there silently, paralyzed. You've been looking forward to this moment for weeks. Now, though, you don't know what to say . . . or more like it, you know exactly what you want to say, but it just seems too stupid, too personal, too embarrassing. So many people have probably asked him these same things—you don't want to put him through it again. You wrack your brain trying to think of the perfect thing to say. You don't want to miss out on this opportunity. But nothing seems good enough.

Come on. There's not much time left. Just say something, anything. It's not like he's going to yell at you if he thinks your question's stupid, you tell yourself. But then the thought of raising your hand and speaking up in front of everyone makes your heart race. Your hands grow moist. Your mouth feels drier than the Sahara. Your stomach ties up in knots.

The class period's almost up. The flood of questions slows. The actor sneaks a peek at his watch. The teacher thanks him, and the bell rings. Your classmates rush to the front for autographs, but you have no desire to be part of the crowd. You don't want to disappear into a horde of dumb fans. Even silence is better than their juvenile behavior. By holding back, you'll seem much more mature and serious than your starry-eyed peers. You're still hoping to get up there and slip in your question at the last minute. Too late! He gets up, shakes the teacher's hand, grabs his coat, and is whisked away by his entourage.

Now the classroom's deserted. You hang back, brooding about your unasked question. You replay the scene in your mind, kicking yourself for wasting this awesome opportunity that'll probably never come around again. You're furious at yourself. In fact, your fear of speaking up is gnawing at you even more than missing out on the career advice you might have gotten from him. Until now your shyness has been at best a personality quirk, and at worst a source of embarrassment. But now it's really interfered with your life. You've really let yourself down this time. If you've gotten to this point in your real life, it's time to make a change.

fight or flight

It'd be a lot easier to talk in front of a group without all the random physical symptoms that go along with shyness, right? The dry mouth, the racing heartbeat—all of that is your brain telling your body that you're in a threatening situation. It's trying to kick you into high gear so that if the threat happened to be, say, a giant grizzly bear, you could run double-time in the other direction. The brain just doesn't get the fact that you can't run away from your English class.

Different people have different shyness symptoms. Some bite their nails when they're nervous. Some tremble, others blush, and still others get sweaty palms. Some experience vocal-chord rebellion, where their voices come out all warbly and off-pitch. And a few especially lucky ones stutter.

While any one of these problems is pretty normal, it only adds to your self-consciousness and makes you even more afraid to speak up. Once you've endured one quavery-voiced oral presentation accompanied by muffled snickers from your classmates, you're likely to be even more nervous next time, which of course only makes the body stuff worse—an endless cycle. But there are things you can do to stop it.

Aha! A member of the silent majority.

you're not alone

First, take comfort in the fact that many of your peers are shy, too. While only about 3.7 percent of people in the United States suffer from social anxiety disorder—a sort of severe kind of shyness that psychologists can diagnose—a whopping 50 percent of people report being shy to the point that it interferes with their lives. And then there's the famous statistic: when asked what they fear most, an overwhelming majority of people said they fear public speaking—even more than they fear death! Countless others become shy only in specific situations, like meeting new people or talking to someone of the opposite sex.

Despite the various triggers for their shyness, there's one characteristic all these bashful people have in common: they all think they're really dumb to feel this way. Still, they can't help it. Why? Because social anxiety goes deeper than your logical mind. You obviously know that raising your hand in class or talking to a hot guy or girl isn't a matter of life and death. It just feels that way. So the well-meaning advice of your friends—picture the class in their underwear, just be yourself—doesn't seem to do any good.

i stutter . . .

Has anything like this ever happened to you? You're sitting in the middle of a row of kids in an auditorium. You've been selected to represent your grade at the state History Day festival. Your job is to explain to everyone in attendance your class's project: an exploration of farming culture and practices of the Middle Ages. You know the subject so well you could talk about it upside-down and backward—alone in your bedroom, that is. You get up when your name is

m . . . m . . . me?

called and read off your speech as though you had a mouthful of Cocoa Puffs. They make you repeat several parts. It doesn't come out any better the second time around. Nor, um, the third. Your voice dwindles, quavers, then shoots up three octaves. You have no breath left to finish your sentence. Every paragraph is like pulling teeth, and the words lose all meaning.

i'm clumsy . . .

Or maybe for you, it goes something like this: A dentist appointment that can't be postponed forces you to leave class in the middle of sixth period. When the time comes, you try to act natural, casual, but you're betrayed by the objects around you. Your chair crashes backward with a smack. Your bag spills open all over the floor. Mortified, you gather up your stuff and attempt to get out of there as quickly as possible. But you stumble, of course, tripping over the leg of the person behind you—much to everyone's amusement. If someone had offered you a glass of water, you would have somehow managed to dump it over your own head.

i blush . . .

Do you see yourself in this story? Last week, your friend Joey lost a special pen that his older sister had given him as a gift. He asked you if, by any chance, you had found it at your house, since he'd come over one night to do homework. As you were telling him that you hadn't seen it, you felt a sudden flash of heat surge outward from your body's core, spread along your neck, your cheeks, and your forehead, then travel outward toward the tips of your ears. Joey looked surprised. Right away, you said to yourself: *I must seem suspicious. Really, though, I haven't seen the pen.* The idea that Joey might suspect you've got the pen makes you blush an even deeper shade of scarlet.

When you are in any kind of awkward situation, you're so anxious that you'll blush that, of course, you do! When someone introduces you

to a stranger, you burst into a lobster-like crimson. When someone asks you a question, you turn into a tomato. When you have to support your point of view in front of someone with a different opinion, you blaze fire-engine red.

Blushing's a biggie for shy folks. Medically speaking, it's called ereuthophobia, from the root word ereuthos, meaning red. It's been plaguing everyone from little girls to old men since just about forever. As soon as emotion attacks, extra blood flows to the face, causing a red appearance. The good news is that, even though you think to yourself, *It's obvious! The other person sees it. He's knows I'm embarrassed and he's going to take advantage of it,* that's not always the case. Not every hot rush you feel results in a shade of red that everyone else notices.

Oh what . . . this? Well, red's my favorite color, so . . .

Which is a good thing, because it's a tough problem to cure. Neither willpower nor any miracle drug has been shown to work on blushing. The best thing to do? Accept that it's a part of you. Seriously! Consider it an innate component of your personality. When you feel the redness coming on, tell the people you're with what you're thinking: "Thanks for the compliment—look, you're making me blush!" or "I'm sure you can tell from my face that you're making me uncomfortable." Letting the other person know what you think about the situation makes him or her assume some of the responsibility for your distress. And by acknowledging your symptom in this way, you're taking yourself out of the position of inferiority—you're saying, "Yeah, I know I'm blushing, it's no big deal." Blushing will just become one of the charming little things that makes you *you*!

i tremble . . .

Like stuttering and blushing, trembling is another one of the outward signs of distress that shy people sometimes show. It's visible in the sheet of paper that quivers when you read aloud in front of the class, and the scrawly letters that replace your normal penmanship when you've got to write on the chalkboard. Tremblers are convinced that others see only the shaking hands. They don't dare raise their eyes to the audience, since they firmly believe everyone's silently laughing at them.

Here again, there's no radical cure. As with blushing, the thought that it might happen makes it more likely to happen. But it is possible to get a more steady hand by practicing relaxation techniques (see page 93) and by putting your motor skills to work through activities that require precision and concentration: do-it-yourself projects, knitting, or archery, for example (see page 83). These will also help tame most of the other physical problems stemming from shyness: sweats, stomach butterflies, heart palpitations, difficulty swallowing, disordered thoughts, stuttering, memory lapses, clumsiness, and tics (such as half-consciously twiddling with your pen or tapping your foot)—just to name a few.

criticism vs.

And for dessert, a delicious tart made by our own culinary queen, Sarah!

You probably devote more energy to tearing yourself down (both in your mind and outwardly to others) than you do to building yourself up. If someone gives you a compliment, you find a way to downplay what you've done: "Oh, well, I don't really deserve an award for my project. My grandpa had a book in his library on army ant socialization; all I had to do was summarize it. . . . "

Shy people are champs at thinking negative thoughts. These thoughts reflect not only how they think they're viewed by others—whom they imagine to be harsher and more disparaging than they actually are—but also how they view themselves. We're our own worst critics.

compliments

This lack of self-esteem might be so deeply ingrained that it seems easier to accept criticism than praise. Good reviews leave shy people ill at ease—they think the reviewer is either lying or mistaken, that they don't really deserve the accolades they're receiving. But when they get bad reviews, they believe they've earned them, because they confirm the poor opinion they hold of themselves. There are no judges more merciless toward themselves than shy people. They remember their failures more vividly than their successes. Their fiascoes were inevitable; their triumphs just dumb luck for which they weren't truly responsible.

Why is it so hard to say "Thank you" or "I'm glad you liked it" in response to a compliment? Is it so impossible to believe that people might like you, even admire you, for who you are and what you do?

How does such a poor self-image take shape? Sometimes, it starts in childhood. Your parents or siblings might have said things like "You can't do anything right!" or "You're just like your father—incapable of managing anything by yourself." Even if they're not said maliciously, they can wound you deeply, sometimes without your knowing it. If this was the case for you, try to recall these early criticisms and put them in proper perspective. React to them, say out loud that they're not true, vow to not live up to them, rather than allow them to gnaw away at you. Whoever said them was probably having serious problems of his or her own at the time—it was about his or her own shortcomings, not yours.

finding the right
balance

Of course, there are times when you'll have to face legitimate criticism—when your English teacher reprimands you for never doing the reading on time, or when you get yelled at for being impolite to dinner guests because you've had a bad day.

This kind of everyday disapproval can hit shy people harder than most. They feel shame more deeply—they're not only ashamed of what they've done wrong, but also of their reactions, their symptoms, of not being like the others, of being a disappointment to those around them.

Feeling humiliated in front of others is hard for anybody. It affects your self-image—for a long time and very deeply. The path to building, or rebuilding, self-esteem is difficult but essential. You must learn to like yourself enough to allow yourself to be liked and respected by others. Learn to listen to criticism, determine whether it's constructive and, if it is, decide what you can do to improve in the future. If it's meant only to be hurtful, try your best to disregard it, to see it as the other person's problem. Everyone possesses the ingredients needed for balanced self-esteem: respect for yourself, awareness of your own desires, knowledge of your strengths and weaknesses, and a willingness to act without fear of failure or being judged.

You just have to find the happy medium somewhere between conceit and humility, the place where you don't think you're better than every-one, but you don't think you're worse, either. That's the secret to healthy self-esteem.

mr. (or ms.) sensitive

Like we said earlier, part of the problem is that you're super-sensitive to others' reactions to you—or, we should say, your perception of how others are reacting. When you see on someone's face even the slightest inkling of surprise, disagreement, or disapproval, you instantly feel rejected and pathetic—like you can't do anything right. You're convinced that things that make others amusing or attractive only make you look ridiculous. If you were to go so far as to tell a joke that you found hilarious coming from your cousin the other day, it would fall flat coming from you. No one would think it's funny, and they'd probably all secretly feel sorry for you.

from flight to fight

Speaking of looks from others . . . they can produce an almost animal-like reaction. In fact, biologists have observed that an unwavering stare automatically triggers defensive reflexes in mammals. Why would humans be any different? Scientists have shown that being "stared down" by another person elicits feelings of discomfort,

anxiety, and even anger in subjects. Standing up to such a look can feel impossible to the shy person.

However, some shy people turn their fear into aggression when they feel threatened—whether knowingly or not. Rather than run away with their tails between their legs, they go on the offensive, shooting menacing looks of their own. Where other shy, insecure people might keep their voices barely above a whisper, the aggressive type turns loud and obnoxious. Afraid their opinions don't matter, they figure saying them loudly enough will force the people around them to listen. Often when those who've kept quiet for so long finally do decide to launch into a speech, it comes out in a single burst, like a diver plunging into the deep end without weighing the risks of the splash he'll make. If you let your insecurity build up like this, the words that finally do come out may prove tactless and get you into trouble. Again, you must find the happy medium between always holding back and letting go completely.

no one notices me

For most shy people (other than maybe the aggressive types), a major consequence of being so timid is the feeling of invisibility. In the hallways, in class, and at parties, they often feel that people are looking right through them, like they don't even exist.

The restaurant waiter ignores your desperate attempts to get his attention so you can order your Coke. When he finally does take your order, he brings you a tomato juice, which, of course, you accept without protest (even

I have things to say.

Me, too!

Am I invisible?

Don't [ig]nore me.

though you hate tomato juice) for fear that he will snap at you instead of admitting his error. So, instead of speaking up, you take what you were given—and probably even tip the guy, too.

At school, it's the same scenario: The few times you actually dare to raise your hand, the teacher scans the class without seeing you. You haven't participated in so long, he's stopped looking toward your corner of the room. But maybe there's one teacher who seems to understand—she never picks on you when you don't volunteer, but always notices and calls on you when you do. You might remember her tripping over her words a bit back at the beginning of the year when she had to face the twenty-eight new pairs of eyes all focused on her. Could she be shy, too? But her condition obviously didn't keep her from doing her student teaching and taking her teacher-certification exam. Actually, the world is full of formerly shy people who have learned to overcome their anxiety and have gone on to lead great, happy lives.

left out and looked at

While you might feel that others are always excluding you from the group, think for a second about whether you might be the one excluding yourself in some situations—times when you could easily have joined the group, yet you purposely hung back. Picture it: When school gets out, everyone meets up at the pizza place or arcade or wherever. But no one specifically says, "Hey, come with us," so you head home alone instead. But walking by all those sidewalk tables filled with your class-

Pizza Palace

Don't look at them . . .
Don't look at them . . .
Don't look at them . . .

mates is like torture. It feels like everyone's eyes are on you, scrutinizing you. You don't know how to act, what kind of attitude to take. You start walking with an awkward, deliberate stride, straight as a rod and without looking at anyone. But you can't shake the feeling that everyone's eyes are fixed on you as if you were a specimen in a microscope.

In situations like these, you have to remember: You're not the only person in the universe, and not everyone is focusing on you 24/7! They're more likely focusing on themselves, just like you are. But to avoid the matter altogether, next time when school gets out, why not just continue the conversation you were having with your chemistry partner as the bell rang and casually say, "Hey, wanna go grab a slice with everyone?" Only an extremely rude (or busy) person would say no.

the wrong impression . . .

Unfortunately, shyness sometimes seems like arrogance to other people. They recognize that you're a smart, decent-looking person, but they see you keeping to yourself all the time, not sharing your unique qualities with those around you. They don't realize it's because shy people like you are often afraid that if they do come out of their shells, they won't measure up. You choose to stay silent rather than fall below the mark. But this sort of perfectionism only hurts you in the long run.

Think about whether you're placing the bar too high. When you try to live up to some extremely high standard—set either by yourself or maybe your family—you can't help but continually feel that you're falling short. Trying to be a saint or a genius or Miss America, maybe all at the same time, simultaneously fosters an overwhelming desire to make a good impression and a panicky fear of not being successful. Any goals that you set for yourself become Mission Impossible.

Well, no one is expected to be perfect. Every person is entitled to take a few steps in the dark, to make mistakes and ultimately learn from them. Knowing how to pick out the lessons from your botched efforts is the key. Doing this requires that you don't wallow in your failures, secretly glad that you proved what you suspected all along—that you aren't good enough. Instead, you've got to pick yourself up, dust yourself off, and set out to try again, using the knowledge you gained from the first go-round.

Remember, choosing silence over self-expression can make others think that you consider yourself "above" participating. Or it may just make them think you've got nothing much going on up there; nothing to say. In many cases, it's better to at least say something than to just stay quiet. All the outgoing people are doing is saying what's in their heads, giving others their opinion—and you should feel free to do the same. Someone might disagree with you, but he's just expressing an opinion, the same as you are.

people act for me

Your friends and family might think they're doing you a favor by speaking up for you all the time, but really, this doesn't help. Because you've gotten so accustomed to them being there to guide you through the world, you never have any motivation to change, to become more independent.

Your best friend is always there to drag you along to parties. She goes with you to the store to help choose your clothes. Without her, you'd feel obligated to buy something from every salesperson who pressured you. You'd end up wearing a down parka in the middle of summer! Your mom still goes with you to the doctor and relays to him what you're feeling in the back of your throat or the pit of your stomach. The only responses you can seem to muster to his questions are blank looks or a shake of your head. If Mom weren't there, you'd probably go home with two aspirin to treat a case of appendicitis!

The relationship between a shy person and his friends and family is like that between a foreigner and his translator. Unable to communicate yourself, you let those around you rush to your aid, speaking for you or doing things on your behalf. So you never learn the basic skills of interacting with others—and, by the way, you're forced to live life according to someone else's interpretations. It turns into a vicious

cycle: The shy become the perpetually inept, who constantly require assistance so that they can be spared any bit of normal, everyday anxiety. Don't let it get this far. Start acting for yourself now, and little by little, the situations that used to make you squirm will start to seem like no big deal.

merciless
judges

For many shy people, the outside world seems populated with enemies whose sole purpose is to lie in wait for their failures. When you were little, you were all on equal footing, but now—with a few exceptions, like your one or two best friends—it seems like your peers have morphed into vicious cannibals, ready to chop you into edible scraps at the slightest provocation.

Take gym class. Maybe the other kids crack jokes about your gracefulness (or lack thereof) on the balance beam. You'd never think to shut them up by recounting the bungee-jumping adventures you had over summer vacation. You know inside that that was a lot more daring than a few pirouettes on the beam. But the idea of speaking up, of confronting them—that seems scarier than launching yourself off that bridge last summer. You'd rather let them think you're incapable than reply to their jeering.

Few people are fond of confrontation. But situations like this hardly qualify. You don't have to make a big deal of it—you don't even have to let them know you were hurt by their teasing. Just make a joke of it: "Yeah, well, apparently I'm going to have to settle for the silver at the Olympics this summer." It's normal to be intimidated by certain people, but it's not as if your classmates are any more extraordinary than you are. They're not famous like the actor who came to your English class. They're not world-reknowned gymnasts themselves. (If they were, they wouldn't dream of making fun of your efforts.) Keep telling yourself this when you feel anxious around them—they're regular people, just like you.

They're not the judge and jury in a court where you're on trial, nor are they your enemies on the battlefield, their sole purpose to annihilate you. Obviously there are some mean people who are out to hurt others. But you have your own life; your reason for being is not to serve as their punching bag. The shy have an unfortunate tendency to believe that the entire earth is concentrating its attention on them alone, conspiring to make them look ridiculous. But that's just not true. And this mix of self-absorption and feelings of persecution is poisonous. Recognizing this is the first step along the path to healing.

the opposite
sex

You have enough problems making friends; how are you ever going to get a boyfriend or girlfriend?

We know right now it seems impossible. Say there's a boy you find attractive. You'd never be courageous enough to approach him, even if it were just to ask the time! Every day, you ride the same bus from the same stop. And every morning, he's there beside you, waiting at the edge of the same sidewalk. Every morning, you tell yourself it's stupid not to start a conversation. But, every morning, when you finally make eye contact, you turn away instantly—you don't want him to think you were looking at him! He must think you're stuck up for not talking—which bothers you, but not enough to give you the backbone to say something.

Here's your first step: Just smile. You don't even have to open your mouth. The way things usually go, one smile elicits another. And once you become two people who smile at each other, "hey" or "what's up" is bound to slip out of one of you eventually. Then one day, you'll graduate to something like "The bus is taking forever today, huh?" A simple exchange of words, no matter how insignificant, is that first spark that leads to getting to know someone. And then, even if things don't go any further, you've at least made an effort. You at least have a new acquaintance and can wait for the bus without feeling tense every day. You can't be attractive to everyone in the world, and you'll have plenty more opportunities to meet people in the near future.

opening up . . .

If you're lucky, your shyness has made you a great listener. People think of you as a good friend, someone they can count on. Since you don't like to talk a lot, you're always ready to listen to others' crises and dramas, both the little everyday stuff and the more serious stuff, and to come to their aid. In difficult situations, people will start to come to you for help, which makes you feel useful and worthwhile.

It's that next step that's probably harder for you. You've opened the door a little by listening. The other person will likely want to open it

wider, to understand you better. The urge you feel to step back, to push that person away, is called a defense mechanism. You're afraid that if you let someone in, tell them your inner thoughts, fears, and feelings, that they'll finally see the real you and not like him. But you've got to take that risk—it's the only way people ever become closer. Try to remember how you reacted when your new friend opened up to you. You didn't think he or she was crazy or weird or inferior. If anything, you probably thought, "Hey, I feel like that, too, sometimes." Letting someone see your good points and your bad points doesn't drive people away—it solidifies your friendship.

If a guy or girl you are interested in starts talking to you about a class, you know how to deal with that. But if the conversation veers off into more personal areas, panic sets in. The conversational tone has

Ball bearings? Oh yeah, you've got a few different kinds: the basic ones, the 608 ABs—they're OK, then the 608 Zs and ZZs—their steel covers make them impermeable to dust. You've also got the 608 Ds and the 608 DDs, which are protected by rubber gaskets. You've also got to take into account the ABEC standard, which determines bearing precision quality. It's on a scale from 1 to 5. ABEC 5, that's the best! It's really straightforward. Do you want me to draw you a picture?

been altered! The two of you are moving from practical matters to flirtation, where you feel completely out of your depth. So you try to escape.

But the thing is, the best place to escape to is the comfort of a relationship. Who else but a friend or a boyfriend or girlfriend can understand you, lend you confidence by supporting you in your moments of self-doubt? Mistrust of everything and everyone can only lead to isolation and loneliness. Accepting the hand that's offered to you—a smile, a kind word—and giving it back in return is the key to feeling loved and accepted.

making progress, but . . .

Let's assume at this point that despite your reluctance, your blushing, your stammering, you've finally made initial contact with someone. Your heart's pounding in your chest, you're short of breath, you're palms are sweaty. That's all normal for everyone. He (or she) smiles, mentions he's got to pick up some new replacement parts for his old roller blades. So you latch onto that and go into a lecture about ball bearings. A voice inside you says, "What are you doing? Ball bearings?? This is not what you talk to your crush about!" He'll think that they're like your major passion in life, when really you just saw a show about them on the home improvement network. But you can't stop rattling on—now that you've started talking, you can't risk clamming back up again and creating that terrible, awkward silence. Maybe if you're lucky, he'll put you out of your misery by kissing you . . .

slogging on

Let's say, hope against hope, he hasn't run screaming for the exit yet and you've been seeing each other for a whole week. Feel free to bounce off the walls in glee for a bit, or entertain fantasies of him as your knight in shining armor, rescuing you from your lonely tower and living with you happily ever after. But try to take things slowly—

to victory!

you're not getting married just yet. Remember your tendency to have both unrealistic expectations and visions of failure. Try to stay in the here and now, enjoy his company, and see him for the person he really is. It might work out, or you might realize you don't have much in common. But either way, the experience is worthwhile.

worst-case

Often, shy people let their imaginations get the better of them. They continually second-guess themselves and the people around them. For example, when the teacher asks a question in class, do you ever say to yourself, "I think I know the answer, but it seems way too easy. It's probably a trick question. And even if it's not, everyone else probably knows the answer, too, and if I raise my hand and give my dumb, obvious answer, everyone will laugh or think I'm trying to show off." Or maybe one boring afternoon you think, "If I ask Jesse to go to the movies with me, she'll probably tell me she can't because she's got to watch her little brother, which I'm sure isn't true." Anticipating problems is, of course, not always a bad thing. We all instinctively try to protect ourselves against the sometimes hostile outside world. In

scenarios

certain circumstances, after sensing a premonition of danger and evading it, you can congratulate yourself on your intuition and be glad you avoided the problem. But anticipating problems everywhere can get you into trouble. If you assume that every opportunity might be a trap, every friendly face a disguise for someone who's out to get you, you'll never go anywhere. You'll be paralyzed. And you'll develop a really dark view of other people—that they're all mean, deceptive, and untrustworthy. The truth is that most things are just what they seem, and most people are on the up and up. It's OK to hold onto a healthy amount of skepticism—you don't want to be gullible—but unless there's really strong evidence to the contrary, give people the benefit of the doubt.

over-thinking

All of us possess a mental VCR that we use to analyze past events—shy people like to keep theirs plugged in 24/7. Instead of taking action to fix whatever happened or resolving to act differently in the future, you spend your time blaming yourself for what you didn't (or did) do. You rewind the tape and replay the scene from different angles, kicking yourself when you realize, in hindsight, exactly what you should have said and lamenting the fact that it's too late now. Train yourself to recognize this thought process in your brain as soon as it's set in motion, then do the best you can to shut it down immediately. This aptitude for overanalyzing the past instead of moving forward is one of the shy person's biggest pitfalls. It's that whole learning-from-your-mistakes thing again. Right now, you're not taking notes on that videotape, you're just replaying it and making yourself feel worse. You're telling yourself, "With me, it's always like that! I'll never be able to [fill in the blank]." You worry about other people judging you, but you're already the champ at that yourself. You pull back into your shell: "I should have shot back so and so, just like such and such, who always gets out of things with some funny comment." These are just empty regrets that don't help you improve anything—unless, of course, they're the beginnings of a real challenge you're laying down for yourself, the prelude to some new resolutions that you're truly willing to work toward. Every event can teach you something about how you want to behave in the future. So play the tape, pick out the lesson, then hit stop. Turn off the

things

mental VCR, walk out the front door and go back to real life with that
lesson in your back pocket.

OK, so it's not that easy. But try to think of it as an athlete would. If
a soccer goalie spent a whole game regretting the goal she'd just let in,

the opposing team would take advantage of that and score again. Everyone needs to get back in position and back in the game. If a tennis player got obsessed about every ball he hit out of bounds, he'd be too preoccupied to smack the next incoming ball back across the net. Inside the locker room at halftime, coaches always tell their players to forget what happened in the first half and play the second half with all the energy and spirit they would at the start of a brand new game.

The situations you encounter in life aren't any different. Accept failure as temporary, then shift gears to focus on the next challenge.

relief at having
kept quiet

A mental VCR that replays negative events isn't the shy person's only problem. Another obstacle for you to overcome might be a sense of relief at having said or done nothing. Even though you're frustrated, sometimes you can't help but feel that a weight has been lifted off your chest when your silence helps you make it through a situation unscathed. You think, "Whew, it's over . . . at least I didn't embarrass myself too badly. I'll remember that next time—that it's safer if I just keep my mouth shut."

You're right, it certainly is safer. But it won't make you happy in the long run. The problem lies in potentially developing what's called a per-

Make sure you're headed in the right direction.

sonality of avoidance. The fear of being criticized, of not being good enough, of seeming ridiculous, crushes any initiative you'd otherwise take. When this happens, any excuse you come up with will do: "It's not worth the effort," you tell yourself, or "I can't go to the party, I've got a hangnail."

Acting on reflex like this can lead only to withdrawal and isolation. You're trying to avoid conflict and anxiety — but as a result, you're missing out on the pleasure of adventure and of potential success. Living this way, everything is orderly and predictable, but there's no enthusiasm or joy. Besides, the little cocoon you've built is likely to be fragile. A failing grade on an exam, a divorce in the family, a romantic rejection—any random happening in life can cause it to break apart. Then it's "Hello, depression!"

Nothing comes without risk. You make friends, you make enemies . . . it's all just a part of life.

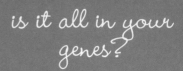
is it all in your genes?

WHY

GROWING PAINS

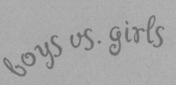
boys vs. girls

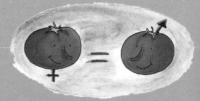

the new kid on the block

PHYSICAL
DIFFERENCES

AM I SHY?

YOUNGER-CHILD SYNDROME

a problem of
heredity?

Maybe your mother says that it's the family curse. Your grand-mother was just like you: terrified by a casual visit from relatives, by the idea of having to ask for something, or by the need to start an argument. She chose to keep quiet, or else to have someone a little more animated do the talking for her. Your mom's temperament is similar—so maybe it's all genetics.

According to some studies, parents who exhibit shyness as a char-acter trait usually have children with the same personality. Researchers wondered if this was because shyness rubbed off on kids during child-hood, or if it was the result of heredity. To figure it out, some researchers focused on twins: identical twins, who share the same genes, and fraternal twins, who do not. These twins shared the same home environ-ment, yet the identical twins were more likely than the fraternal twins to have the same shy characteristic, thus indicating that genes are a factor in shyness. In fact, children of shy parents reportedly have a 40 percent chance of being shy themselves.

Studies of families of monkeys have yielded similar conclusions. Finally, researchers purposely bred laboratory mice from pairs of mother and father mice that shared signs of anxiety and avoidance behaviors. The result was the creation of a whole family of timid mice!

the irritable
amygdala

Some scientists, attempting to further explain the development of shyness, have studied infants and their behavior with their mothers. Many babies exhibit anxiety when they're in unusual situations or among strangers. These infants become agitated and show signs of fright—an accelerated heart rhythm and dilation of the pupils. But instead of revealing early-onset shyness, this behavior is actually just a normal, temporary stage of infants' psychological development. Many babies appear mistrustful, and even afraid, of faces not familiar to them. A significant number of them cry to express their unhappiness at being separated from the people who normally care for them. This is just a signal that they've grown up enough to recognize their parents' faces,

Sure, I'll take another shot of hormones.

but not enough to understand that when Mom and Dad leave, they will come back. Since this is true for all babies, scientists have a fairly difficult time studying shyness in kids this age and declaring that a particular baby has been born shier than another.

Some experts, on the other hand, have been successful at showing that certain people are predisposed—that is, more likely—to turn out shier than others. One researcher at Harvard University believes that shyness is anchored in a region of the brain called the cerebral amygdala. This part appears to be especially sensitive in timid people, reacting strongly to the everyday occurrences of life and triggering intense emotions. (Unfortunately, it's not something you can elect to have surgically removed!) Located in the limbic area of your brain, it goes off when fired upon by certain powerful neurotransmitters, the

hormones called serotonin, adrenaline, and noradrenaline. The interaction between these substances and an irritable amygdala might be partly to blame for the fact that you come apart at the seams much more easily than, say, your little brother. While you and your siblings have similar genes since you have common ancestors, none are exactly alike, so you might have inherited some traits that your siblings didn't, and vice versa.

But let's stop just a second. You shouldn't throw your hands up in the air and say, "Well, I am the way I am! That's just how I was made." You may, indeed, have been predisposed by your genes to be the timid type; however, that doesn't mean your life is predetermined. You were dealt this hand of cards, but only you decide how you're going to play it.

a problem of
adolescence?

For some time now, you've been changing so quickly that soon you may not even recognize yourself. In fact, doctors confirm that during no other period of life does the human body change as much or as quickly as it does in adolescence. Between the ages of eleven and fourteen, it can almost double its weight (from 75 to 150 pounds for boys, from 65 to 130 for girls) and grow a good several inches per year. At the same time, the sex organs are also developing, bringing on a whole slew

I'm covered with zits, my butt is enormous, I've got ears like Dumbo, my clothes are ugly, I'm failing school, and I sure as heck don't have a boyfriend . . .

But yeah, everything's fine!

of additional changes. In barely four or five years, we completely change our skins, so to speak, becoming entirely different young men and women. Obviously, it's not easy going through such a huge physical upheaval. So it's not surprising that some kids start to hate their new bodies before they have a chance to grow into them and get used to them.

Like those feet, for example! They seem like real boats when you match them up next to those tiny little-kid shoes they fit into only a year ago. And the hair—on the arms, legs, and other unimaginable places—what good does that do anyone? And for the girls: hips that are way softer and fleshier than before, and breasts that are getting so big they're starting to look like udders! If this keeps up, making chest traps at soccer practice is going to get a lot harder. Boys might be a little more optimistic about some parts of their physical transformation, like the broadening of their shoulders and the muscle development. But they'll likely have a harder time with the body hair and the high-pitched fluctuations of a breaking voice, not to mention the acne.

Try to remember when your shy feelings first showed up. Have you always been quiet, or is it something relatively new? Maybe you've heard your parents say that when you were little, you were funny and uninhibited. You'd go up to any stranger on the beach or at the grocery store. Everyone laughed at your clowning around and the silly things that came out of your mouth. You were the focus of everyone's attention. Maybe it wasn't until adolescence—with the acne, the awareness of physical or intellectual flaws, anxiety about the future, and the first stirrings of infatuation with the opposite sex—that your personality took a turn. Or, perhaps you were always naturally introverted, but as you grew, you became more and more withdrawn.

As a shy child, people probably thought you were fairly cute—it was OK to hide behind your parents when meeting new people. But as a teenager, that kind of thing doesn't fly. But it's not like things got to be this way overnight. Social anxiety grows stronger and puts down roots over time—and middle school and high school are perfect environments for it to flourish. As a kid, you kind of had the right to be bashful: You could be untalkative, refuse to say hello sometimes, hide in the back room . . . . Now, suddenly, as an adolescent, this is seen as immature, and you're doubly punished for it. Your parents say things like, "You actually brooded for an entire week over not getting your money back from that kid you lent it to? You couldn't just ask him?" And then there are the harsh predictions: "The way you are, your first job interview certainly won't be easy." They pigeonhole you as the stereotypical

She won't let us? Usually she's afraid to say no. . . .

person who will never succeed on her own. Don't they realize that's not doing anything for your self-esteem?

As for you, you probably think, quite rightly, that you're not the only one responsible for these predicaments. That kid could have had the courtesy to return the money he borrowed so you wouldn't have to ask for it. But the thing is, you can't change the behavior of others. You can only choose your own actions. So there will always be times when you've got to stand up for yourself. All you have to do is pick up the phone, ask politely for what you want, and be able to say "no" if the other person suggests something unacceptable to you. People won't like you any less because of it—in fact, they'll respect you more for being assertive than for being a pushover.

And isn't that what it's all about for you? You keep quiet because you're afraid of not being accepted. You desperately want to be liked at all costs. You'd rather just take whatever people give you than raise objections or ask for what you need. The ironic thing is that trying to please everyone will not necessarily gain you respect.

is it a matter of
upbringing?

Is there someone in your family—say, a cousin—who's much more outgoing and seems to succeed at everything? She had the same timid grandmother as you, yet, despite this genetic inheritance, her parents didn't raise her in exactly the same way yours raised you. Maybe your uncle is more emotionally assertive than your father, who's a model of decorum. Your uncle might be quicker to anger, but also more forthcoming with the compliments, and, when his daughter deserves it, he makes it known that he's proud of her. Your father, on the other hand, is quite the opposite. His sense of modesty prevents him from expressing his annoyances, his joys, and his tenderness, even though he definitely feels these things. Your aunt, too, is probably different from your mother. Perhaps she's a little more relaxed; if your cousin doesn't do well at something, your aunt finds excuses for her and doesn't bombard her with reprimands. So your cousin never really has her abilities called into question—how could she not be self-confident?

If your parents always try to act in everyone's best interest, you probably feel obliged to do the same. And if your mother offers the slightest criticism or your father retreats into a disapproving silence, you feel you've let them down. Surely they don't purposefully disavow or ignore your accomplishments, but all the same, you might like a little more praise and encouragement. Because of their rebukes, even the justifiable ones, you feel that they're more aware of your weaknesses

than your strengths. So you strive even harder to be a good kid, to be on your best behavior in every situation. Don't say anything, don't open your mouth. It's the very mature child who prefers getting things because he deserves them, rather than by screaming demands and stomping his feet. But unfortunately, sometimes the squeaky wheel gets the oil—that is, you might have been so well-behaved that after a while people forgot to notice and praise you for it. You don't go looking for compliments, because you'd rather they flow naturally when you've earned them. You're certainly justified to think that way. But remember— you can only change your own actions, not others'. So next time you're feeling unappreciated, give them a hint by saying something like, "Hey Mom, did you like the painting I did for the art show?" And know that, regardless of the disapproval they sometimes express—or the approval they sometimes forget to express—your parents love you just as you are.

is gender the
culprit?

Are girls shier than boys? For a long time people valued reserve in girls and manly daring in boys. This is still the case in many countries. Even in the United States, up to the beginning of the twentieth century, it was thought that girls should hold their tongues, while courage, self-assurance, and decisiveness were the qualities looked for in boys. When they didn't conform to these rules, girls were considered insolent and obnoxious, and boys cowardly and faint-hearted.

But all that's different today. Social anxiety is something that affects both sexes. Girls are no longer expected to obey a stereotype that demands perfect self-control. However, even though we now enjoy greater gender equality, there are still some people who hold onto old-fashioned ideas—for example, thinking that men should always be tough, or that women can't be good at business because they're too emotional or polite. But the gap narrows more and more every day.

Plenty of girls raise their hands in class, express their opinions, ask boys out, and participate in athletic competition. And quiet, sensitive boys feel free to write poems or play the guitar instead of picking fights on the playground. In fact, they're often thought of as "handsome, dark brooders" or "strong, silent types." The extroverts aren't always the ones who get the girls.

is it a feeling of social
inferiority?

Is that hypothetical cousin of yours who always seems so self-confident by any chance wealthier as well? Maybe when you were children, you adored her because she always had new clothes or new stories of cute boys or vacations or fancy parties. Sure, you had a greater imagination, and you were the one who always invented the games you played together. But she was the one who commanded: "I'll be the queen and you'll be my servant." While you didn't always love the role, it did seem to fit you. You'd never have dreamed of being the queen. You would have been embarrassed; imaginary power didn't interest you any more than real power does now.

If this rings true for you, you might notice a similar pattern with the people who currently make you feel most anxious or timid. It could be a friend whose parents both have incredible jobs, whose house is bigger

This summer, I'm going to Europe for a month with my parents, then two weeks in Australia with Chloe . . . How fantastic is that?! And what're you doing?

than yours, or who lives in a better neighborhood. She wears only the best, most expensive brands. And when she invites you over, you feel like a total slob, like you have to be careful not to let on that you bought your shoes on sale and your underwear from a supermarket.

Feeling inferior makes some people launch into a furious competition and others become self-conscious and hide their true selves by shying away. Neither is a great choice. What you need to remember in this type of situation is that having more stuff doesn't make anyone nicer, smarter, or friendlier. If the well-to-do people look down on you, they're missing out on having you for a friend. On the other hand, if they ask you to hang out, they obviously like you for who you are—not how big your TV is—so you can feel comfortable letting them see the real you. Being happy with what you have is a tough thing to learn, and some people never quite get it. But it does become easier to appreciate your blessings as you get older.

culture shock

Having a native language, religion, customs, and/or a physical appearance that differs from those of the people around you can make you feel really isolated. And the disconnect between what happens at school and the way things are at home can be confusing and frustrating.

Racism and ignorance of different cultures on the part of some of your classmates or community members probably doesn't help. Fortunately, this is becoming less and less common and prejudice will, with luck, one day be a thing of the past. Many high schools now have multicultural clubs dedi-

cated to improving understanding, as well as bilingual classes to help new kids adjust. Music, movies, and sports are way ahead of the curve, with performers and athletes of all colors being appreciated by audiences made up of the same.

appearances

Quite likely, whatever your ethnic or cultural origin, you don't feel ecstatic about your looks right now. Most teenagers are merciless in front of a mirror. You think this part is too fat, this part too skinny. You're too short, too tall, too misshapen. You're too weird looking, or even too normal. You wish you had hair like that girl's, arms like that guy's, and skin that could go a day without erupting.

In addition to this self-criticism, most young people are also convinced that others notice every little flaw and hold it against them. We all sometimes wish that we could just be invisible but, the way shy people hang back out of the crowd, some just might get their wish.

Rest assured that whatever body part you're obsessing about, it's way more noticeable to you than to anyone else. And, ironically, others probably recognize the good parts about you way more readily than you do your-self. The truth is, nobody is perfect. Everyone has some feature they're not so fond of. If, even after acknowledging this, you still feel like your supposed flaw is truly significant, there's always something you can do about it. There are hundreds of products designed to clear up acne—and a hundred more for covering it up. Learning what clothes accentuate the parts you like and hide the ones you don't can help. Joining a gym or a sports team, or even talking to your doc-tor can be a first step toward sculpting a healthier body. And then there's atti-tude. Plenty of people who aren't supermodel gorgeous are considered extremely attractive because of their unique personalities. With a little humor and self-deprecation (that is, willingness to laugh at yourself), you can draw others toward you instead of pushing them away.

Physical beauty is subjective. Our idea of what looks good changes over time and from place to place. What some find ugly, others find irresistible. But kindness and charm are universal—they will always be in style.

what if i'm
disabled?

When you're stricken with a major physical disability, whether the problem started at birth or resulted from a disease or an accident, relating to others is trickier. Many associations exist to support young disabled people and their parents. Major informational campaigns have been launched in the media to open people's minds. Every public school and most public buildings are required to accommodate wheelchairs. Competitions like the Special Olympics have been organized to provide an outlet to showcase your abilities and to provide examples of willpower and courage to guide you. There's no shortage of inspiration in the performing arts with numerous blind singers and deaf actors finding fame. If they had shied away from the spotlight because of their differences, they'd have missed out on some incredible experiences, and we'd be missing out on some incredible performances.

a specific

event?

Some people who were never particularly shy before grew to be that way following specific events that affected their whole lives.

One example would be if your parents had to move the family to a new place because of work, landing you in a new town without any friends. It's one thing to make friends when you're five years old, but it's a whole other thing when you're suddenly the new kid on the block. Because you were forced to entertain yourself for a while, you might have developed a taste for solitude. You got out of the habit of dealing with other kids.

Other examples would be moving in with stepbrothers and stepsisters, or going away to boarding school. You probably felt as though you were dropped into a hostile, alien world. Old feelings of shyness that you thought you'd overcome may have returned—that instinctual fear of going against habit and wandering off from a place of security to explore a world teeming with mysteries, perils, and troubles. Once you get used to this new place, though, it'll seem much less foreign and scary. You might even find that there are some things about your new life that you like better than your old life.

As for situations like summer camp or boarding school, these are actually some of the easiest places to meet new people without too much stress. At least a quarter of all the kids there will be new, just like you, so they'll be just as nervous, and just as eager to hook up with new friends.

As for divorce, that's not easy for anyone. Separation and the breakup of a family are painful, and often lead to a lot of introspection and, therefore, withdrawal into oneself. In your mind, the divorce may have revived your fear of being less loved. Your mother's or father's new spouse and his or her children may have intruded into your personal space and messed up your routine. But after a period of healing, acceptance, and getting used to each other, your feelings of balance and security will return. If you're lucky, you'll get the brother or sister you never had, and come out stronger and happier on the other side.

a new birth?

Anybody in there?

When your little brother was born, you thought he was cute, just like everyone else, right? But then maybe, to everyone else, he started seeming more interesting than you, funnier than you, less stubborn than you. Was it around then that you started hiding in the bathroom anytime a strange car pulled up out front? If your parents eventually began to compare the two of you—and never in your favor—that was likely the last straw.

Becoming the older kid in a traditional family or one that includes stepchildren often has an effect on your self-esteem. Jealousy, frustration, and a feeling that things aren't fair are all too common—and they can touch off, once again, this feeling of inadequacy. The ability to adapt to a new position in the family depends somewhat on the parents' handling of the situation, but also on each individual's capacity to deal with change. In fact, for some, becoming the big brother or sister—and therefore the biggest, strongest, smartest, and most responsible—actually increases their sense of self-worth.

other types of
sibling rivalry

You don't have to be the oldest to have trouble with brothers and sisters. Babies of the family often feel like they're second best at everything. Your older brother or sister has always led the way, has always been stronger, a better artist or writer, and the star athlete. You were the little kid whom your sibling could crush with his superior strength and knowledge. Statistics show that older and only children who were showered with their parents' attention are often more self-confident and perform better than the younger ones. They tend to be independent and super-responsible.

However, your position as youngest child does have its advantages! Parents sometimes put less pressure to succeed on their youngest as opposed to their oldest. And once the oldest child has "broken in" his parents, the youngest has fewer rules to follow and less severe punishments when he breaks the few there are! The position of last-born may, in fact, be pretty cushy, since parents tend to spoil their last baby bird in the nest. Just try not to abuse it. Living a sheltered life by letting Mom do everything for you will only put you at a disadvantage once you hit high school and college and have to make your own way.

Being an only child also has its ups and downs. You obviously have none of the sibling rivalry and conflict bigger families do. On the other hand, "lonely onlies" have fewer opportunities to learn to tolerate the personalities of other people, and they may harbor a feeling of isolation that leads to shyness. Shy kids without sisters and brothers should try to take advantage of opportunities to interact with other people their age; for example, sleepovers, team sports, summer camps, visits to see cousins, and stuff like that. We know—those are exactly the kind of situations that make you nervous! But if you can make yourself participate at least a little bit, you'll be glad you did.

Some experts believe that the way you fit into the fabric of the family has a big influence on your personality. You're not living in a vacuum, and your psychological makeup is not set in stone. We all evolve over time, according to the environment, events, and the way the members of our little group relate to one another. A million and one things can affect the way a family develops over time, gently—and sometimes not so gently—molding and shaping the people in it. Depending on the circumstances, these factors might lead a person to slip back into shyness, or they might help her finally open up.

So what if one of your siblings is stealing your thunder at the moment. It doesn't mean he or she will always be the only shining star. The expression "slow and steady wins the race" is true not only in long-distance running, but in life. Take your time, be patient and persistent and you're bound to make all the right moves. If your big moment hasn't come yet, it just means that you still have your greatest accomplishments to look forward to.

dear diary . . .

WHAT CAN I

ACT THE PART

THE
DOCTOR
IS IN

move it
or lose it

play that
funky music

DO ABOUT IT?

just BREATHE

adjust your
attitude

First of all, you have to realize that your shyness is disrupting your daily life and that you gain nothing by telling yourself: "I can't do anything about it. That's just how I am. I can't change." Avoiding the situations that you find nerve-wracking will only make the problem worse, freezing into your mind the idea that you can't handle them. Life is full of surprises, and each person, including you, has a unique gift. All you have to do is identify and cultivate it, then dare to use it to assert your personality.

In fact, you can use this gift to change the way others look at you. That "shy" sign you've got pinned to your back? Tear it into pieces. Forget about all the mistakes and missteps of the past and focus on the present. Or, use those experiences as a source of inspiration and pride—think about everything you've gotten through to bring you to where you are today!

Julia,

a writing
assignment

Try on another side of your personality. Say you've suffered through years of hand-me-downs instead of new clothes of your own, and coming up on the new school year, things aren't looking to be any different this time around. Instead of silently stewing about it, why not furiously scribble out your feelings on paper, maybe even throwing in a subtle, sarcastic joke here and there? If you could get up the courage to read your "Ode to My Pants, Two Sizes Too Big" out loud to your parents, they might start to see you in a new light. OK, so they won't think you're suddenly the life of the party—people don't change overnight—but you might start to become known for your deadpan wit. And you might get some new pants out of the deal.

Taking things at face value isn't usually the shy person's strong suit; you tend to overanalyze and take everything seriously—on occasion, tragically. Off-the-cuff repartee probably isn't your thing either, since the confidence to say whatever pops into your head isn't typically part of your temperament.

As a result, writing may be a mode of expression that flows more easily for you than speech. The solitude and time required for writing suit you better. Faced with a blank page, you'll have more time to weigh your words, rework your sentences, and instill a tone of sincerity, emotion, or amusement, depending on what you're going for.

Among other forms of writing, keeping a diary may allow you to learn more about yourself. You'll be able to pick apart what makes you tick, analyze the day's events, and release the tensions that those events produced. You never know: Your thoughts might even interest others. Writing —either conveying what you wouldn't have the nerve to say out loud, or tackling more literary projects—will enable you to probe your own thoughts and give them some organization. You'll be able to vent any emotions you've kept hidden inside and relieve the stress they bring.

Writing classes and clubs are becoming more and more common at schools and community centers. Joining one allows you to compare what you've written to the works of others and often take part in group writing projects under the supervision of actual authors or skilled coaches.

studio arts

What if you—unbelievable as it seems—were to perfect your drawing technique to the point where your art teacher thought it would be a great idea to show your work at an exhibition? It's not as unlikely as it sounds!

All of the studio arts (drawing, painting, sculpture, photography, and many others) can be practiced alone or at studios, in the company of people who share this same passion. When you're working alongside others, it's easier to strike up relationships, since a great potential topic of conversation is right there in front of you. Regular school art classes might not offer this same opportunity, but signing up for a special class offered by a local college or community center can be a great way to meet new people. You'll learn together, compare your work, and exchange techniques. Through artistic pursuits, you can express the universe of emotion you keep secret inside you and have trouble communicating to others. You'll be able to show your talent to your friends and family, or in individual or group exhibitions. Mastering a brush stroke or potter's wheel can also help a butterfingers or a trembler gain a more steady hand.

dance,
ice skating . . .

Suppose that, through your work at the barre, your flexibility exercises, and your repeated plies, you, the distant, unapproachable one, were to outdo yourself at the dance recital?

Dancing allows you to become acutely aware of your body, to sculpt it, to feel at ease inside it, and then to take possession of the

Bravo!

Bravo!

Bravo!

gymnastics,

surrounding space—it can do wonders for your self-esteem, instilling a sense of beauty and grace. Besides its effects on the body, the effort it wrings from your muscles, and the fluidity and agility it bestows, dance counts among the most entertaining of the arts, giving joy to the viewer and true gratification to the performer. It's also something you do both alone and as an essential part of a group, requiring you to put in hours of hard work with your team, building camaraderie. However, the world of dance can also be competitive, especially ballet. If you are truly motivated and, above all, perseverant, you'll be able to stick it out and climb the ranks from student to extra—and maybe even to prima ballerina!

If you're just looking for some fun on a Friday night, sign up for a social dancing class like salsa. On the other hand, if you like the creativity of dance but want something a little more sporty, think about ice skating or gymnastics. All of these offer similar psychological—and social—benefits.

singing

Admit it: You sing in the shower. Or the car. Or pretty much anywhere there's a radio on and no one else around. You probably never thought about letting anyone hear you, but if you're honest with yourself, you might realize you actually have a pretty decent voice.

Singing develops and strengthens the voice and teaches breath control. Since expressing oneself out loud is difficult for the shy person, singing can be an excellent way for you to free yourself from your hang-ups and assert yourself. And, like the other activities we've mentioned so far, it's a great way to both interact with other people (as part of a chorus or choir) and to release some tension.

music

So you've decided for sure that the only audience suitable for your singing is your rubber ducky? There are other ways to get music into your life. Playing an instrument also opens the way toward personal development and communication with others. Learning to play is some-times slow and grueling—at first, sheet music seems like a foreign language. But it actually will give you entrée into a new way of express-ing yourself other than speech. Piano, recorder, violin, saxophone, harpsichord, electric guitar, synthesizer, organ, accordion, drums, etc.

— you can choose among an infinite number of instruments from all eras, continents, and cultures. After the initial learning stage, practicing becomes a lot more fun. And after weeks of rehearsals, performance in public (even if you do feel a little stage fright) will give you intense satisfaction and a sense that you've finally overcome your shyness. And that can't help but bump up your self-esteem. And it's not like you have to become a soloist. Being part of a band or an orchestra will nourish your sense of belonging, of sharing, and of participating in an extraordinary event.

horseback riding

Welcome to the club!

Imagine if, after countless turns around the ring, tumbles into the sawdust, and hours of training, you got the blue ribbon at a horse show! Horseback riding combines athleticism, the love of an animal, and outdoor activity. While simply walking your horse at first isn't as exciting as your first attempts at running and jumping will be, it allows you to get to know your mount and become accustomed to his personality and behavior. This may be the perfect activity for the super-shy, since you don't have to talk much to the other riders in your class. You'll have fun taking trail rides together, feeling the wind and the sensation of freedom—then maybe while you're tacking up one day, you'll all start chatting. During competitions, you'll have the opportunity to perform, to feel the satisfaction of surmounting obstacles and the joy of triumphing over your rivals—and your own insecurities. It's just another way of coming to understand your full worth and showing it off!

team sports

This natural remedy for the shy—physical exertion and train-ing—works with all sports, but in particular team sports, which strengthen cooperation within a group.

There's a team sport for all tastes. Whether you prefer handball to basketball, soccer to rugby, or volleyball to ice hockey, it's up to you! The most important thing is to place your skills, energy, and willpower at the service of the team you've chosen. Even sports that put the focus on the individual, such as track and field, tennis, and fencing, require that you participate under the team's banner.

Attending a game as a player or even as a spectator allows you to share in the common spirit—when a goal is scored or a point won, it's contagious and irresistible. In triumph and disappointment, victory and defeat, you can't help but join together with your fellow teammates or ticket holders.

the
martial arts

From judo to kung fu, but not leaving out karate, Aikido, and kendo, among others, there are about seventy-five martial arts sports taught today. Here, too, the choice is yours. By channeling ener-gy and emphasizing self-control and respect for the opponent, these sports combine physical mastery with increased concentration and focus. As with other disciplines, joining a club where you train regularly encourages you to get out and meet people.

Other Eastern traditions include yoga and tai chi, both of which are especially suited for shy people. Yoga's aim is harmony of body and mind. There are many kinds of yoga, but all put an emphasis on controlled breathing and "chi," the life force. The intense stretching; deep, abdominal breathing; and psychic relaxation practiced in yoga will help you release your tensions.

Compared to other, harsher disciplines, tai chi is all about fluidity of mind and motion, as well as, again, the life force, known as chi. It can be adapted to your body type, your preoccupations, and the personal quest you're on. The slow, purposeful movements done in tai chi will enhance your awareness of your own body, making it seem more like a powerful instrument than a burden. You invest your entire being in every pose, right down to your fingertips. Tai chi can be practiced alone or in a group where everyone's movements are coordinated, helping to connect and tune you in to those around you.

theater

It sounds crazy, we know—but imagine standing up on stage in front of the whole school and absolutely nailing your performance as a lead in *Romeo and Juliet,* bringing the house down and earning a standing ovation. With a little practice, it's not such a far-out prospect, even for someone who gets stage fright just talking in front of a couple of friends.

In fact, theater is actually a very effective way to fight your freeze-ups. You've got to face your fears head-on, right? Acting and improvisation classes work to improve voice and breath control, diction, memory, physical presence, and movement, all of which, in turn, help you to feel relaxed and comfortable in your own skin. Getting up on stage for rehearsals every day slowly chips away at your fear of appearing in front of others, whether it's kids at school or an occasionally larger audience.

And if it turns out that you happen to be especially talented, you might even get a new career direction out of it. Even if you're content to remain an amateur, you can still use your dramatic skills—a clear voice, improved vocal delivery, poise, and self-assurance—for oral presentations, job interviews, or just entertaining the crowd during lunch in the cafeteria. Lastly, some of the fictional situations that you'll see played out on the stage (conflicts, love scenes, explosions of joy or anger) may come up in your own life, and you might just be better equipped to handle them having role-played through them once already.

relaxation
therapy

Relaxation therapy is something that can help you feel more at ease. It can be practiced regularly at home, on your own, and then called upon when you need to calm your nerves in social situations. You can take classes to learn the techniques, hire a therapist to coach you through it, or learn on your own. It involves working on the body and mind by combining the benefits of yoga (bodily awareness, breathing, and mental concentration) with meditation. There are several different approaches. One is called progressive relaxation, where you tense and relax each muscle group, one at a time—your feet, your calves, your thighs, your abdomen, your fists, your arms, your shoulders, etc.—until all the tension is gone from your body. Another approach is simple meditation, where you sit quietly, and focus on taking deep breaths through the nose—in and out, in and out, until your mind is clear and your body is relaxed. A third approach is to combine these two methods then add in a mantra—a word or phrase, such as "om" or "tranquility" or anything else that works for you, which you repeat over and over to help clear your mind even further.

Once you've mastered the ability to relax your mind and body in the privacy of your own room, you can use this skill out in the real world. For example, while you're sitting in class waiting for your turn to give a presentation, take note of what your body is doing—are your shoulders all hunched up by your ears? Is your heart racing? Take those slow, deep breaths you've been practicing and see if you can slow down your pulse, and with each exhale, feel your shoulders slump down a little farther till they're back where they're supposed to be.

Relaxation therapy doesn't only help you de-stress in scary situations; it'll help your overall attitude as well. When you achieve this harmony of body and mind after continuous practice, your anxieties and symptoms will decrease in intensity. You'll be able to gain more control of your emotions, express yourself more effectively, and understand what's going on in and around you. By reducing your inner and outer conflicts, it will also enhance your relationships with friends, parents, and teachers. By strengthening your self-confidence and self-esteem, you'll be free to believe in your potential.

professional
help

If you've worked hard to try to overcome your feelings of shyness but they're still interfering with your life and your happiness, you might consider seeing a psychologist. You can find one through your school guidance counselor, or the phone book, or online, but since therapy is something you probably can't afford yourself, the best thing to do is probably to ask your parents.

Once you've found someone you feel comfortable with, he or she will try to help you break the pattern of your shy behavior. Over time, your brain gets conditioned to automatically react the same way in certain situations, just like your dog does, directing him to offer his paw whenever you stick your hand out. If you want your brain (or your dog's) to react differently, you have to retrain it. The therapist will have you tell him what's bothering you and what you'd like to change. Then the two of you will agree to work together to accomplish that goal. He'll help you to understand that your social anxiety is likely due in part to the misperception in your head that everyone is noticing everything you do and that they're all harshly judging you for it—neither of which is true. He'll

counsel you to move your focus away from your discomfort and take an interest in the people in front of you instead. He might also use a technique called "systematic desensitization," which helps you gradually become less sensitive to the things that make you nervous. First, you write down all of the situations in which you're shy or anxious, in order from the least stressful to the most stressful—for example, talking to a classmate, meeting a new person, talking to a guy or girl you like, giving an oral report, and performing on stage. Then you'll imagine being in the first situation, and use breathing and relaxation techniques you've learned to calm yourself down. After practicing in a therapy session, you'll try out the situation in real life. If you no longer feel shy in that first, least-stressful situation, you'll move on to the next situation on your list, and so forth.

We're shy, we're proud, we're getting loud.

This process can take a couple months to become effective. But during that time you'll make progress little by little, becoming more and more confident as the weeks pass. The therapist will probably have you write down the positive feelings and outcomes that result from your improvement—all part of the brain's retraining process.

Not that the goal is to have you thinking good thoughts till they make you sick, or to feel so confident that you become conceited or obnoxious. A happy medium is what you're striving for.

Of course, this method focuses more on the symptoms of your shyness than the underlying cause. But during your sessions, your therapist will also ask questions to help you get to the root of the problem, so you've got an even better shot at solving it for good.

medication

Unfortunately, there's no miracle pill for shyness. You don't treat it the same way you would indigestion or the flu. However, if social anxiety is taking over your life and you've tried therapy for some time with no improvement, there are certain drugs a psychiatrist can prescribe to help. They affect the chemicals in your brain, and so must be used very cautiously and, preferably, for a limited period of time.

First, there's a class of drugs called beta blockers, which are used to treat cardiovascular disease. Doctors have noticed that they also effectively decrease some of the physical symptoms of anxiety, such as trembling, sweating, and rapid heart rate. They're called beta blockers because they act on tiny parts of the brain known as beta-receptors that welcome stress hormones. Beta blockers weaken the effect of these hormones. Your doctor might choose to prescribe them to you before a big event, such as a performance, presentation, or major exam to help calm your nerves.

However, these drugs don't solve the basic problem—they won't turn a shy person into a Broadway star. They merely provide one-time assistance that you may be able to call upon under extraordinary circumstances. Just like illegal drugs and alcohol, abusing them can be dangerous.

While these substances give the temporary illusion of relaxation and/or euphoria, relying on them to function just makes matters worse.

That said, one other class of drugs, antidepressants, are in fact prescribed for more long-term use to treat extreme shyness. The antidepressant Paxil, for instance, was recently approved by the Food and Drug Administration (FDA) as a treatment for social anxiety disorder. Going on medication is a very serious decision that you and your doctor will make together if you both feel it's right for you and other treatment options have proven ineffective. Again, these drugs are not a cure-all, and may not work for everyone.

there is hope!

Social anxiety isn't just something you can "get over" like outgoing people think, and it causes real pain to those who suffer from it. But like most problems in life, you can overcome it. The simple fact of realizing that you're not alone—that adults who are now seemingly self-confident once went through the same ordeal—should encourage you. The courage and the perseverance needed to open yourself up to a new way of thinking might even make you stronger than you would have been otherwise. The fear you feel is deep-seated and has developed over time; it won't go away overnight. But every time you raise your hand in class, every time you call a new friend, every time you stand up in front of others to express your opinion, you're one step closer to living the life you want.

Don't worry . . .
we'll get through it . . .

BOOKS TO READ

The Relaxation & Stress Reduction Workbook, by Martha Davis, Matthew McKay, Ph.D., and Elizabeth Robbins Eshelman (New Harbinger Publications, 2000)

Instant Calm: Over 100 Easy-to-Use Techniques for Relaxing Mind and Body, by Paul Wilson (Plume, 1999)

Conquering Shyness: The Battle Anyone Can Win, by Jonathan Cheek, Ph.D. (Dell, 1990)

Painfully Shy: How to Overcome Social Anxiety and Reclaim Your Life, by Barbara Markway, Ph.D., and Greg Markway, Ph.D. (Thomas Dunne Books, 2003)

Triumph Over Shyness: Conquering Shyness and Social Anxiety, by Murray B. Stein and John R. Walker (McGraw-Hill/Contemporary Books, 2001)

How To Start a Conversation and Make Friends, by Don Gabor (Fireside, 2001)

10 Simple Solutions to Shyness: How to Overcome Shyness, Social Anxiety, & Fear of Public Speaking, by Martin M. Antony, Ph.D. (New Harbinger Publications, 2004)

USEFUL WEBSITES

Anxiety Disorders Association of America
www.adaa.org
Clearinghouse of information about anxiety disorders,
including social anxiety. Learn more, take a screening test,
and find a therapist near you.

anxietycoach.com
A self-help guide with techniques for improving public speaking,
stage fright, and social phobia.

Kidshealth.com
Social anxiety information, written especially for young people.
Enter the teen section of the site, then click on "Your Mind," then
"Social Phobia."

The National Women's Health Information Center
www.nimh.nih.gov/publicat/phobiafacts.cfm
Facts on social phobia, including its symptoms, possible causes
and treatments. (Even though this site is dedicated to women's
health, the anxiety information applies to guys, too.)

GoAskAlice.com
Frank and honest Q&A site run by Columbia University. Click on the
"emotional health" link, then on the "stress & anxiety" section.

BIBLIOGRAPHY

Statistics:
www.nimh.nih.gov/publicat/phobiafacts.cfm

www.shyness.com

Therapy/medication info:
Dr. Jonathan Cheek, Ph.D.
Department of Psychology
Wellesley College

Index

A

acknowledging symptoms of shyness, 22

actions, choosing your, 61, 63

adolescence impact on shyness, 58–61, 68–69

adrenaline, 57

aggressive shy people, 29–30

amygdala, cerebral, 56–57

anticipating problems (symptom of shyness), 46–47

antidepressants for shyness, 100

appearance, impact on shyness, 58–61, 68–69

arrogance vs. shyness, 33–34

attitude adjustment for dealing with shyness, 80, 95

avoidance personality, 50–51

B

balanced self-esteem, 27–28

beta blockers for shyness, 99–100

blaming yourself (symptom of shyness), 48–50

blushing (ereuthophobia) (symptom of shyness), 20–22

boarding school, shyness about, 72

books on shyness, 102

boys vs. girls, 64–65

brain and shyness, 56–57, 96, 98, 99

breathing techniques for dealing with shyness, 93, 95, 97

C

cerebral amygdala, 56–57

childhood experiences, impact on shyness, 26, 62–63

clumsiness (symptom of shyness), 19, 23

confrontation, fear of (symptom of shyness), 38–39

constructive criticism, 27–28

criticism vs. compliments, 24–28

culture, impact on shyness, 67

D

dance for dealing with shyness, 84–85

dealing with shyness, 80–105

actions, choosing your, 61, 63

antidepressants, 100

attitude adjustment, 80, 95

beta blockers, 99–100

books on shyness, 102

breathing techniques, 93, 95, 97

dance, 84–85

desensitization technique, 97

diary, 82

drugs, 99–100

gymnastics, 85

horseback riding, 88

ice skating, 85

journaling, 82

mantras, 93

martial arts, 89–90

medication, 99–100

meditation, 93

motor skills development, 23, 83–84

music, 86–87

perseverance, 101

professional help, 95–98

progressive relaxation, 93

relaxation therapy, 23, 93–95, 97

self-deprecation, 69

singing, 86

about the authors

Melissa Daly is a former senior staff writer at *Seventeen,* where she wrote about sex, health, and relationships. She is currently associate editor at *Fitness* and she also writes for *YM* and *Weekly Reader.* She holds a degree in psychology from the College of William & Mary.

Claude Clément writes for teenagers. She is the author of *The Word Without Which Nothing Exists*, published by Sorbier. Having overcome her own shyness, she is glad to be able to help teens do the same.